I0040477

THE HALO EFFECT

HIGH-PERFORMING, AGILE, LEARNING ORGANIZATIONS©

JERRY TARASOFSKY

This book is presented solely for educational and motivational purposes. Although the author and publisher have made every effort to ensure that the information in this book was correct at press time, the author and publisher do not assume and hereby disclaim any liability to any party for any loss, damage, or disruption caused by errors or omissions, whether such errors or omissions result from negligence, accident, or any other cause.

THE HALO EFFECT Copyright © 2017 by Jerry Tarasofsky. All rights reserved. Printed in Canada. No part of this book may be used or reproduced in any manner whatsoever without written permission except in the case of brief quotations embodied in critical articles and reviews. For information, address PPS Publishing 3-1750 The Queensway Suite 1312 Toronto ON M9C 5H5.

PPS Publishing books may be purchased for educational, business, or sales promotional use. For information, please email the Special Markets Department at SPsales@ppspublishing.com.

Published by PPS Publishing www.ppspublishing.com

PPS PUB

3-1750 The Queensway Suite 1312 Toronto Ontario M9C 5H5

ISBN (Print): 978-1-988994-03-1

ISBN (eBook): 978-1-988994-04-8

10 9 8 7 6 5 4 3 2 1

DEDICATED TO THE MEMORY OF

MAX GARFINKLE Ph.D.

Max, passed away on November 26, 1999. He was my business partner in the development of this methodology. He was ahead of his time, and like him The HALO Effect for understanding and creating High-performing, Agile, Learning Organizations© methodology is more comprehensive and empowering than anything else available, even today.

Like the human DNA, *the* capabilities *of an organization differentiate it from every other organization and influence its growth, development, functioning, health and success.*

The road to becoming a HALO *is predicated on quantifying those Essential Capabilities that are critical to the successful operational performance of every organization.*

TABLE OF CONTENTS

AN IDEAL ORGANIZATION VISION

People create organizations. These organizations are the vehicles of their ambition to reach a goal, whether financial or other. Whether they are financially or otherwise motivated, the beginnings of organizations are outcomes of the drive and ambition of individuals.

Many enterprises start. Some last for a while. Few, however, endure for decades. What are the factors that allow some organizations to survive over the long term?

People have dreams, or are driven by needs often related to their survival, or the betterment of their personal and/or family situation. Very often, without necessarily being aware, they set out to attain that end. It is the first step in the process of becoming what they want to become. It usually takes sacrifice, personal determination and perseverance. Whatever the means, the trigger is an aim, a plan, a goal, a vision.

If as a result, they create a business or a non-profit organization, their vision is their driving force. Usually, those organizations that can sustain growth for a period are either the result of the drive of the original founder(s) or the buy-in to the vision by others that join it.

In our Meta review of the literature (reference our Research in Appendix 5), we recognized three characteristics of those organizations that had been able to sustain long-term success. They all had visions that contained the same key elements: higher performance, agility, and a learning environment.

We coined the acronym **HALO** for Higher-performing, Agile, Learning Organizations©.

A HALO is an ideal-striving organization that aims for the ideal of **continuous renewal**. Continuous renewal results from the integration of the processes of improvement, adaptation, innovation, and development. Each process complements and supplements the other processes. The actions of a HALO keep the organization on its journey of continuous renewal.

So, in our terminology, **HALO represents an ideal-striving organization seeking continuous renewal.**

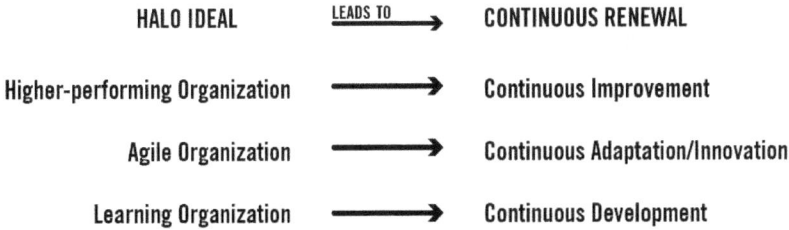

HALO IDEAL	LEADS TO →	CONTINUOUS RENEWAL
Higher-performing Organization	→	Continuous Improvement
Agile Organization	→	Continuous Adaptation/Innovation
Learning Organization	→	Continuous Development

HALO and continuous renewal are process ideals. The distinction between a process ideal and one tied to specific content is illustrated by the saying: "Give a man a fish and he has food for one day. Teach him how to fish and he has food for a lifetime." Superior students achieve their results by striving toward the process-ideal of learning-how-to-learn.

If you could wish for anything in the world, what would you wish for? The best answer is the process-ideal: "I would wish that all my future wishes will come true." If you could wish for any type of organization, what would you wish for? The best answer is the process-ideal, **"I would wish for a HALO that is always striving for continuous renewal."**

The process-ideal of continuous renewal by being a HALO serves as a direction for organization action, not as an endpoint. While ideals are ultimate standards, they are never 100% attainable.

A HALO is an ideal-striving organization, not an ideal organization.

Every organization should be challenged for continuous renewal. The workforce should be dedicated to striving for the organization that "could be" rather than to maintaining what "is". All the people in the organization need to be mobilized to overcome complacency, fight rigid bureaucracy and resist mediocrity.

The next generation of effective organizations will be continuously evolving and capable of transforming themselves to survive and prosper.

The ultimate purposes of any type of organization can be more readily achieved when a program of continuous renewal has been instituted. Both large and small businesses are concerned with creating higher profits by beating the competition. Not-for-profit organizations, such as health care, educational and public service institutions, are concerned with realizing their mission by offering superior value to their clientele. All can benefit from becoming a HALO and sustaining a process of continuous renewal.

The following illustrates the basic premise on how the ideal of becoming a HALO and continuously renewing oneself as a HALO can be used to mobilize workforce commitment and change efforts toward greater progress in achieving the organization's purposes.

HALO IDEAL   <u>CONTINUOUS RENEWAL</u>   →   MISSION PROGRESS

SOME EXAMPLES
Higher Profits/increasing Shareholder Value
Superior Customer Value
Lifetime Customer Loyalty
Sustained Competitive Advantage
Enhanced Quality Of Work Life
Innovation In Products And/or Services
Community And Social Responsibility

Striving to become a HALO is the ultimate vision statement for every organization!

Traversing the journey to becoming a HALO, however, is not simple. It requires the ability to always understand your current organizations current strengths and weaknesses. It requires the ability to monitor your progress. It requires the ability to identify issues that may be blocking the way. It requires a way to measure change. It requires a way to guide the process. And it requires the **full** commitment of a determined leadership.

CHAPTER I

TRANSFORMING VISION INTO THE HALO EFFECT

To transform a vision into actionable components, one must begin with the ultimate objective of creating an organization that desires to progress toward the ideal of striving for continuous organization renewal.

As outlined earlier, a continuous organization renewal integrates three desired processes:

A higher performing organization striving for continuous improvement;
An agile organization striving for continuous adaptation to change;
A learning organization striving for continuous development of capabilities.

To attain that ultimate vision, understanding how organizations in general, whether for profit or non-profit function led to creating a unique map for its conceptual framework. This map serves as a guide for organization action towards continuous renewal ideals.

Maps are not the same as models.

Most organization models apply an *analytic approach* for creating knowledge.

Maps however, apply a pragmatic *actors approach* for creating knowledge. Each orientation advocates its own research and application methodology. A map aims for results that are relevant and actionable more than for information that is rigorous and precise.

The map is for the members of an organization who seek to realize their intentions of progress toward their ideals. This map provides the lines of action for a journey of renewal that has milestones but no destination—other than the process ideals of continuous renewal.

The map parallels the commonsense notion that progress depends upon the interaction between effort and ability.

In organizations, the motivational component is referred to as a strategic challenge—a call to action in a strategic area.

The map posits five strategic challenges as long-term objectives towards continuous renewal.

The competence component for organization renewal is referred to as an essential capability.

An essential capability is a combination of *organization practices* and the *capabilities and competencies of those persons involved* that achieves a strategic goal. The map prescribes three essential capabilities for progress in each of the five-strategic challenges. These fifteen essential capabilities are generic in that they apply to any type of organization, regardless of size or mission.

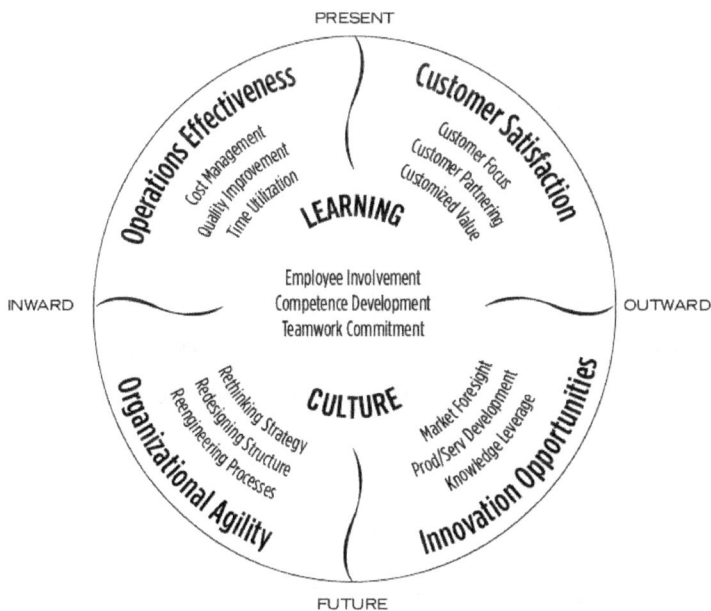

PRESENT

Operations Effectiveness
Cost Management
Quality Improvement
Time Utilization

Customer Satisfaction
Customer Focus
Customer Partnering
Customized Value

LEARNING

Employee Involvement
Competence Development
Teamwork Commitment

INWARD

OUTWARD

Organizational Agility
Rethinking Strategy
Redesigning Structure
Reengineering Processes

CULTURE

Innovation Opportunities
Market Foresight
Prod/Serv Development
Knowledge Leverage

FUTURE

The visual representation of both the Strategic Challenges and Essential Capabilities is reflected above.

The map becomes the shared language of striving for renewal throughout all units, levels and functions of an organization. It provides a common direction of ends to be pursued.

The map converts continuous improvement ideals into long-term objectives [strategic challenges], into short-term goals [essential capabilities] and into the means for achievement [their unique organization practices).

From a timeline perspective, Customer Satisfaction and Operational Effectiveness are basic for any organization to exist—relating to its present state, whereas Organization Agility and Innovation Opportunities are requirements to attain an ongoing future state.

From an orientation perspective, both Operational Effectiveness and Organization Agility are inward *focused* challenges, the control resting within the company, whereas Customer Satisfaction and Innovation Opportunities are both outward *focused*, with external issues and events influencing those challenges.

From an execution perspective, the organization leadership and resulting Learning Culture created by them are the get done *capabilities* required for each of the four others.

When any organization operationalizes the map, the explicit message to respondents is: "tell us to what extent we have succeeded in becoming a higher performing, agile, learning organization. We need to enlist your help in eliminating our weaknesses and building on our strengths."

THE FIVE STRATEGIC CHALLENGES OF ALL ORGANIZATIONS

CUSTOMER SATISFACTION—delivering outstanding value to customers

Everyone understands the value of customer satisfaction. In a Bain & Company study with 362 firms, 80% believed that they delivered a "superior experience" to their customers. But the customer only rated 8% as actually delivered from their perspective. Building relationships and establishing long-term loyalty is difficult. It combines a capability of **focusing** and understanding what customers want; dialoguing and **partnering** with them for their ongoing success and **customizing** products and services to their specific needs.

Your waiter is courteous and friendly, but does not know the ingredients of the dish you are interested in, or needs to go back to the kitchen each time to find out, or takes your finished plate away before your companions have finished theirs, or does not suggest an alternative if the dish you just ordered takes a long time to make even though you requested fast service, or to tell you that that the kitchen is very backlogged, or does not record the special request to keep the sauce separate, and on and on. Is it the waiters fault or that of management?

The training of every person within a company that interacts with a customer is mandatory. How to talk, what to know, how to react to unusual requests, and being updated and aware of all product/services of the company.

Jeff Bezos has driven the art of Customer Satisfaction to such a level that Amazon is rated at the top of the ladder in that category. Did you know that he at times still participates in customer complaint calls, to understand his customers, and learn how to make them happy? He certainly succeeded.

INNOVATION OPPORTUNITIES*—creating and achieving breakthrough innovations*

Innovation (as defined in Wikipedia) is often also viewed as the application of better solutions that meet new requirements, unarticulated needs, or existing market needs. This is accomplished through more effective products, processes, services, technologies, or business models that are readily available to markets, governments and society. The term 'innovation' means something original and more effective and, consequently, new, that 'breaks into' the market or society. It is related to, but not the same as, invention.

Innovation requires an **ongoing developmental** process of improving existing products and services, while developing new ones to expand market share with existing customers, and to develop new customers and markets. It requires **market foresight**—the constant understand of the competition and marketplace and it requires **leveraging knowledge** from both external sources as well as that which exists within the company.

Innovation from within any organization is a primary driver. Encouraging everyone in the company to care about the company can have enormous impact on innovation.

I experienced this firsthand:

When I worked as a summer student for Alcan in their Shawinigan, Quebec smelter, I was placed in charge of the Suggestion Box. At that time, Alcan would pay a multiple of the first year's annual savings, or a percentage the first year's annual sales, for any suggestion that was implemented. I was advised to check it every day, as they had had good experiences with it.

In my first week at the plant, I discovered an envelope in the box, and brought it to the head of engineering, who was my boss.

The letter outlined a design of a ceramic piece that would be attached to the head of the funnel that poured the hot smoldering aluminum that came from the furnace into the cooling silos that were set very deep in the ground. Once cooled, the resulting large and long spherical shaped inqots were removed and sent to their extruding plants that turned them into marketable products such a building siding, windows etc.

The employee, on his own, built one such ceramic head at his home, and offered to have it used. His theory being that with his device, the amount of air that is usually captured during the pouring stage into the ingot, would be reduced. Unbeknown to me, I learned that the bubbles caused by the air in each ingot, often resulted in significant sections of the ingot being scrapped during the extrusion phase.

With his ceramic head, a significant percent of the bubbles were eliminated, greatly increasing the usability of each ingot. This employee motivated initiative saved the company money and gave it a competitive advantage over its competitors.

Start-ups are innovation led. Most believe that their idea can change their industry/the world. And some, like Apple have done just that. Steve Jobs focused his innovation on the user experience, creating a device that democratized technology and made it usable to everyone. Not only did Apple continue to improve its offerings, but opened innovative ways to expand that ability.

For companies to rise above a single innovation into a long-term business means creating a sustainable culture of innovation within the organization.

OPERATIONAL EFFECTIVENESS—doing the right things in the right way

Being able to **manage costs** so that it can be the low-cost provider in its sector and thereby deflecting competition while delivering or exceeding the **quality** standards expected of it, and being as **efficient** as possible are the most important identifiers of an organization that operates most effectively.

These are important productivity functions that all companies would understand and thrive for. However, the challenge is always in keeping it up—the ability to constantly improve in all three areas, as part of its ongoing operations. Developing a sustainable culture to continuously evaluate and improve these key components are essential to long-term success.

Companies that understand this will not need to make sudden large-scale layoffs as they will be consistently be operating at an efficient level. Layoffs and cost cutting to improve profits are short-term strategies which most often impact quality, customers satisfaction, and impact sales, all of which create barriers for growth.

ORGANIZATION AGILITY—*assuring that the organization adopts to change*

Change is a constant. Staying still is a business death scenario. Any strategy undertaken likely will be impacted by many internal and external influences. **Revisiting strategy** is an important task that cannot be ignored.

Agility is also dependent on how adaptive its human capital **structure** is to shifting responsibilities created by changing business needs and directions. Also important is the adaptiveness/**re-engineering** of its technology and systems to, for example, sudden scaling of activity, or integrating with another company, among others.

LEARNING CULTURE—*creating conditions that support continuous learning**

At the heart of every business are its people. Every aspect of any business is influenced by them. **Employee involvement** —getting positively felt participation in their company usually reflects how the leadership cares about their **competence development**. *"I will care about you if you demonstrate that you respect and care about me"* is a hallmark of long-term successful businesses. This includes breaking down silos and turf issues within the company and creating an environment that builds on a **teamwork commitment**—having constructive dialogues within and between departments.

Culture played a key role in the personal experience that I had when I worked at Alcan as described above. The company at that time was not unionized, but it was very employee centric and staff interest in the company's success was very strong. The employee who created that ceramic piece cared enough about the company that had employed him for over 20 years to spend the time and expense in his creation on his own time.

SUMMARY OVERVIEW OF THE HALO EFFECT PROCESS

HALO = HIGHER PERFORMING
AGILE LEARNING

ORGANIZATION: **The ultimate vision
of successful long-term enterprises:**
A higher performing organization
strives for continuous improvement;
An agile organization strives for continuous adaptation to change;
A learning organization strives for continuous development of
capabilities.

A **HALO** enterprise is the result of the actions and interactions
between **5 STRATEGIC CHALLENGES** that are universal for every type
and size of business:
*CUSTOMER SATISFACTION; INNOVATION OPPORTUNITIES;
OPERATIONS EFFECTIVENESS; ORGANIZATION AGILITY, and
LEARNING CULTURE*

Each **STRATEGIC CHALLENGE** being operationalized by the execution
of 3 Essential Capabilities namely:
CUSTOMER SATISFACTION—**Customer Focus, Customer Partnering,
Customized Value**
INNOVATION OPPORTUNITIES—**Product/service Development,
Market Foresight, Knowledge Leverage**
OPERATIONS EFFECTIVENESS—**Cost Management, Quality
Improvement, Time Utilization**

ORGANIZATION AGILITY—**Rethinking Strategy, Re-engineering Processes, Re-designing structure**

LEARNING CULTURE—**Employee Involvement, Competence Development, Teamwork Commitment**

Each **Essential Capability** being the sum of: the organization practices, systems, procedures, policies, programs, methods, habits and routines that make up each one, along with the **competencies of the management and staff** that are involved.

CHAPTER 2

WHAT QUANTIFYING THE HALO EFFECT CAN TELL YOU ABOUT YOUR COMPANY

All commercially operating businesses are complex, and the complexity expands as the business grows. That is due to the infinite variables generated by the mixing of multiple persons—each bringing unique backgrounds, capabilities, interests and needs. Customers, suppliers, managers and employees each contribute to this mixture, along with the organization's operational systems, locations, markets, technologies and products.

Independent of its complexity quantifying its Essential Capabilities provides a way for any type and size of business, including yours, to understand the state of its operational performance criteria that directly influence its FUTURE

financial and growth performance; non-of which are reflected in its Balance Sheet.

Culture: An organization's culture is key to its long-term success. Peter Drucker said that "culture eats strategy for breakfast". But how does a company quantify its culture? How uniform is culture in a company that has multiple departments, divisions and branches? What is a good culture as opposed to one that is not so good? Can diverse cultures survive within the same company? By understanding and quantifying the overall Essential Capabilities of a business, and that of their departments, branches and divisions, you can get a handle on its culture and can therefore make informed decisions related to it.

Customer centricity: Knowing the perspective of your customers on how well you operate your company in all the areas that implicate them, can often be out of alignment with how well you, your management and staff perceive it. Knowing how they, your customers rate your Essential Capabilities raises awareness of where you are, or are not with respect to that alignment.

Management effectiveness is another key to a company's long-term success. You can assess managers' performance on an individual basis and provide resources to improve their skills. Yet it is difficult to have knowledge of the overall effect of their actions on the overall success of the company. The unbiased evaluation of the role of management by management itself, employees, customers and suppliers on the company's Essential Capabilities provides that insight.

The level of engagement in the company of management, employees, customers and suppliers is another key to ensuring a successful future. Understanding to how each of these stakeholders rate the Essential Capabilities of the company, overall, by department, branch and division, provides that insight.

Brand value and **goodwill** play a significant role in any company's future. Although there are subjective methods to have a grasp on these essential elements, there is no way of quantifying them in a universal comparative context. The quantification of its Essential Capabilities provides that.

The innovation orientation of any enterprise is essential for long term growth. Knowledge of its Essential Capabilities will identify any barriers that may limit that ability as well as enhance the creation of a culture of innovation.

Organization change: Driven by the acceleration of technology, the ability of any organization to be able to adapt to change is important. Knowledge of its Essential Capabilities allows you to understand how adaptive your organization is.

In addition to the valuable information that is not quantified in any Balance Sheet, knowledge of the state of the business' Essential Capabilities provides other significant benefits:

SWOT: An understanding of the business' strengths and weaknesses. Historic independent SWOT (strengths, weaknesses, opportunities, threats) analysis methods that were popular in the 50's, 60's and 70's have fallen out of favor, due to their costs, time involved, subjectivity and benchmarking ability.

There are surprisingly no methods available in the marketplace that provide a full 360° comprehensive quantifiable analysis that is efficient and unbiased based on the perceptions of all stakeholders.

The quantitative rating of all its Essential Capabilities by management, employees, customers and suppliers on a common platform is the first methodology that provides a clearly identified and unbiased assessment of the organization's strengths and weaknesses. It does it quickly and economically, providing information that can be acted on to drive improvement.

Monitor change: Based on the constant changes that all organizations experience throughout the journey, having a baseline to reflect on enables leadership to react accordingly. Change can only be validated if measurable metrics are consistent over time. Quantifying the state of your company's Essential Capabilities offers such an ability.

Maintaining the status quo. Even if, according to you, everything in your company is going right, knowing the state of your company's Essential Capabilities and monitoring them is a HEALTH check on the company. It will keep you sensitive to your competitive positioning and provide advanced knowledge that you may not have gained through any other means. It avoids surprises.

The HALO Effect by quantifying the Essential Capabilities of your company helps in understanding root causes of problems, enhances the taking of positive actions, and provides the ability to measure the effectiveness of the actions undertaken.

THE HALO EFFECT IS DISRUPTIVE TO CURRENT BUSINESS IMPROVEMENT APPROACHES.

It is disruptive because there has never been a consistent way to:

• Translate the complexity of business in a way that all stakeholders can understand;

- Quickly and economically do a benchmarkable and comprehensive Strengths, Weaknesses, Opportunities and Threats (SWOT) analysis of an organization.
- Quantify the non-financial performance of any size enterprise without any disruption to their organization;
- Effectively measure and monitor operational performance change;
- Provide an independent qualification of nonfinancial business progress;
- Identify the cause/effect of all key aspects of a activity with the other elements of that business;
- Compare the external perspectives of customers and suppliers with the internal perspectives of management and staff on the exact same parameters;
- Benchmark a company's performance data with that of others in its industry/ sector.

Starting with In Search of Excellence originally published in 1988 by Tom Peters and Robert Waterman; Built to Last in 1991 by Jim Collins and Jerry Porras and Good to Great by Jim Collins in 2001, there have been many books written to analyse successful businesses over the years. In general, these books identified the principles that each company exhibited that attributed to their success at that time.

The HALO Effect methodology would have provided an analytical framework to each company and a way to measure their operational performance, and provide insights to their future potential.

IS APPLE MEASURABLE?

We know that Steve Jobs was a creative genius, and his innovativeness has been significant. But Apple's success goes far beyond Steve's product creativity. Many companies have created innovative products and services, but only a few have transferred that innovation into a long term successful business.

Quantifying its Essential Capabilities allows us to understand how Apple accomplished what it has.

AND WHAT ABOUT AMAZON?

Quantification of its Essential Capabilities provides the theoretical embodiment of the 4 Pillars that Jeff Bezos has intuitively institutionalized in making all his company's so successful. Reference Appendix 1.

Knowing the quantitative value of its Essential Capabilities allows YOUR company to be understood, and be measurable for improvement.

CHAPTER 3:

OUR JOURNEY

The genesis of our research is outlined in Appendix 2. This initiative for this book was stimulated by my observation of multiple enterprises that quantified their Essential Capabilities over several years. In each of the following examples the methodology was successful in contributing to their objectives.

A major global chemical corporation used the methodology to monitor its transformation to a virtual company without compromising customer service, affecting sales, and employee relations.

A mid-market Boston-based manufacturer of restaurant equipment used the methodology to assist with their strategic planning.

A plastics manufacturer used the methodology for several years. Over that period, they transformed a struggling enterprise into a successful business that they could sell

A major Canadian insurance firm successfully used it to help with the integration of a company they had acquired.

A large Private Equity firms used it as part of their due-diligence process for all their targeted acquisitions to enhance their pre-acquisition knowledge.

A major construction conglomerate used it to improve and grow one of their weakest divisions into the top-performing division in their organization. It has since been institutionalized within many of their divisions.

A global enterprise in the health care industry applied it for many years and significantly reduced customer turnover.

How else does one explain how a single resource can accomplish so many things for such a diverse group of organizations of so many types and sizes?

Just as the Human Genome Project mapped out the basic elements of the human body, our research mapped out the key elements of the operating functions of any organization. Just as each human in the world has its own unique map, so does every organization have its own unique map of capabilities.

Much as the X-ray, Cat Scan and MRI are medical resources to see inside our bodies and provide visualization of our functioning and identify the roots of issues that exist within it, this methodology provides the means to identifying the root issues behind an organization's operational performance.

Determining the unique capabilities that would be applicable to every organization also requires major investment and effort on a company-by-company basis; **a virtually impossible task.** Our research initiative, however, enabled us to identify the universal capabilities that operationalize the strategic challenges of any type and size of business.

Leveraging that knowledge, we eliminated the complexity of identifying which unique set of capabilities had to be considered in every different company down to a greatly simplified approach that **universally addresses every company and organization.**

Using basic survey technology and the Internet, quantification of its Essential Capabilities is accomplished through listening to all stakeholder groups that know the company including; customers, suppliers, managers and employees.

The result is a **Keep-It-Simple** approach that turns business complexity into a functional business improvement resource—a way to both see where it is at and help ensure and create its future.

It gives every person, whether a customer, supplier, executive/ manager, and employee, a common language with which to communicate with each other and understand the company in question's essential capabilities.

Unlike the popular organization paradigms that have emerged over the years such as: The Balanced Scorecard, TQM, ISO 9000, Six Sigma, and Lean Manufacturing amongst others, ALL of which are different for each company and cannot be benchmarked as a result, **the approach taken is universally applicable and allows comparisons of change over time.**

CHAPTER 4

KEY FACTORS THAT ARE IMPORTANT FOR THE INTEGRITY OF THE HALO EFFECT PROCESS AND ITS IMPLEMENTATION.

Multisource [360°] feedback

Continuous improvement is nourished by feedback from representatives of all categories of stakeholders. Stakeholders are those persons, both within and outside the organization, that have an interest in the continued well-being and effectiveness of the organization. Stakeholder feedback to the organization creates awareness that can mobilize resources for improvement and development.

Some organizations with a human resource emphasis focus on feedback solely from internal stakeholders—employees and management. Some organizations with a marketing emphasis focus on feedback solely from external stakeholders—customers, suppliers and others within their network of contacts. Quantifying the Essential Capabilities must be based on integrating the feedback from both internal and external stakeholders.

Respect of confidentiality

Participants must be confident that their individual ratings are protected and are fully anonymous. By grouping all internal respondents together by their category, respondents are comforted by the knowledge that their individual opinions are respected and they can be candid in their feedback.

Same questions for everyone

The same questions must be asked of everyone so that the measures can be compared. For example, management may rate its organization high on customer satisfaction while the customer scores are significantly lower or vice-versa. Such discrepancy between one group's perspective and another's become the occasions for organization sense-making. The organization needs to be aware of the extent that its culture is integrated, differentiated, or even fragmented amongst diverse groups of stakeholders.

Quantifying perception

Each participant must be challenged to quantify their perception to the questions. It is natural for those who know the organization to provide a judgment related to the question as it affects the company. However, their experience with other companies will also play a role in their responses, with the responses reflecting how well the participant sees the company's ability in relation to other organizations and experiences that they have had.

An optimal feedback system provides the organization with knowledge that serves as a basis for deciding on strategic and operational priorities. The organization needs to know to what extent its stated or intended strategy is the one perceived by stakeholders in different relationships with it. In addition, the organization needs to hear the voices of all its stakeholders regarding the strengths and weaknesses of its current performance.

The value of customer feedback is particularly significant as it effectively rates their loyalty to the organization, or to the relevant unit of operations, and identifies from their perspective which of the Essential Capabilities they deem to merit improvement and provide value for their ongoing engagement.

The questionnaire

Questionnaires need to be customized to fit the practices and concerns of different industries such as manufacturing, service, distribution and construction.

Group perspectives

All stakeholder respondents need to be asked: "In your opinion, to what extent do you see [XYZ] as an organization that…?". The scoring used allows everyone to select between a range from "poor" to "outstanding".

Based upon subjective experiences with the organization, each respondent gives his/her own subjective perception of organization strength in each of the Essential Capabilities. Each response is a valid opinion for that person, even when objective performance measures may indicate that the opinion may be erroneous.

The scoring defines organization reality as perceived by a respondent at a point in time. These perceptions do count, as they influence the nature of the respondent's ongoing relationship with the organization.

Data needs to be aggregated to proceed from individual perceptions to the identification of perspectives by sub-groups, groups, and stakeholder categories—the combined wisdom of the multiple respondents within each grouping. The distribution of individual scores of members of a group and sub-group are described by group measures of central tendency (e.g. averages).

To overcome a possible tendency by some groups to be overly critical or too generous in their praise, the average scores are converted into rankings. These rankings portray relative standing, highs or lows in comparison to the other scores by that group. Thus, even though all Essential Capabilities rated scores by the Supervisor group seem to be unduly low, the rankings indicate which of the Essential Capabilities scored somewhat better and which scored the worst from this group's perspective.

By articulating diverse viewpoints, it gives each stakeholder group and/or subgroup a language with which to explore the effectiveness of the organization.

Language

Participants must respond in their language of comfort. In a global world, the language employed is therefore vital to assure proper interpretation. However, as the quantifying numeric scale is universal, language does not limit the analysis.

Technology

To be effective and responsive, the quantitative data gathering process must be designed to be easy to implement, execute quickly, be easy to interpret and very economical, overcoming all the usual barriers that have limited organizations from benefiting from the value of similar methodologies.

It becomes a diagnostic resource that can be efficiently and economically re-run periodically to monitor change.

A suggested community dialogue style approach to organization sensemaking—

Striving to become the best requires building consensus regarding the state of current capabilities as well as the lines of action to be taken for improvement and development amongst all stakeholders.

Management, often facilitated by independent counsel, makes sense of the data by focusing on the differences in scores and rankings amongst groups and sub-groups within a stakeholder category, as well as on differences amongst different stakeholder categories. The larger the gap—the more one unit seems to deviate from the norms of the other units—the greater the requirement for sense-making.

The context for discovering the meaning of the data is derived from the comparison of unit perspectives. When independent sources of information obtained during the same time frame tend to agree, there is validity by consensus. For example, if the total samples of all stakeholder entities rank Quality Improvement as the number one Capability, it can be reasonably assumed that this Capability is strong within the organization.

However, when group perspectives differ from one another, it is not possible to automatically determine which perspective is more valid. Disagreements amongst group perspectives serve to enhance rather than diminish the value of the methodology. There are multiple ways of viewing the capabilities of the organization. In seeking to understand the reasons for a group's perspective, the organization can become more responsive to that group.

Just as management collaborates in the process of organization inquiry by customizing the sampling, it also gets involved in the process of organization sense-making. The managers are not passive spectators being handed an interpretation and recommendations for action. These practitioners during on-line situations are the inquirers and sense makers, bringing what they already know as the context for the new knowledge being presented.

The approach thus avoids the two most pervasive problems regarding the utilization of survey research and organization diagnostics, namely, strong resistance to and even rejection of the findings or its opposite of extreme dependency upon the researchers as experts.

Organization sense-making becomes a social activity.

Even in their solitary review of the data managers or those involved, may be anticipating how others will react to these results. Such meetings consist of dialogues in search of shared meanings and common understandings. The collective actions of an organization rest upon alignments that take place during such group communications.

As managers review the data they notice results that surprise them or that support or confirm what they expected to find. Such discrepancies initiate attempts at explanation. Different managers will pick out different cues. These cues may highlight problematic situations and/or organization possibilities.

Managers are pragmatic and favor plausible and reasonable interpretations. The following examples typify the understandings reached by management as they collectively make sense of the data.

Strength: All stakeholder groups rank "Customer Focus" as the top Essential Capability.

Weakness: The two Strategic Challenges pertaining to competing in the future are ranked lowest. [Generating Organization Agility; Realizing Innovation Opportunities]

Threat: Although the average rating of the organization by all 50 customers was good [7.3] the bottom quartile of customers was giving ratings ranging from 3.4 to 5.1. Their responses indicate a high degree of dissatisfaction and potential for switching to the competition.

Opportunity: The low scores on the Essential Capability "Teamwork Commitment" created the opportunity for the organization to launch an intensive program of "Team Development".

THE FLYWHEEL EFFECT

A practical organization change approach originally proposed by Jim Collins in his classic book Good to Great

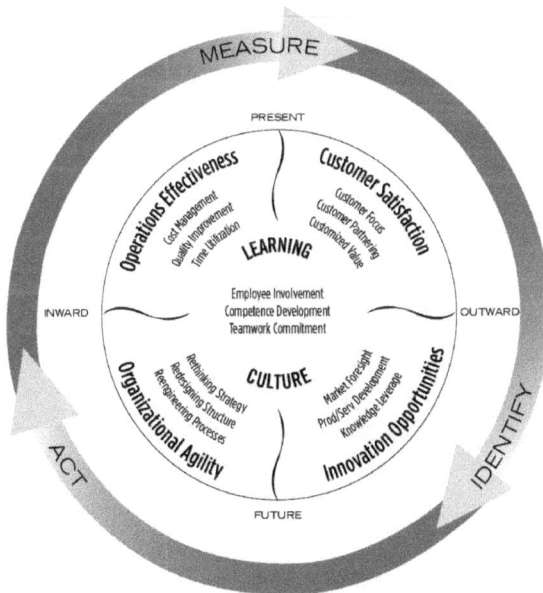

Change is an arduous process and is not an instant one. It's a long-term undertaking, driven by a leadership committed to the process and can take years to accomplish. But as with a flywheel, it is very hard to start, and the first turn is very slow. As the process continues, however, it takes less effort for the second turn, and so forth; eventually the discipline of The HALO Effect creates an organization wide momentum for continuous renewal.

CHAPTER 5

THE LIVING MAP

"Maps apply a pragmatic 'actors approach' for creating knowledge. Each orientation advocates its own research and application methodology."

Although long term successful organization usually begins by emphasizing one strategic challenge orientation, as they evolve that one is re-enforced by all the other four. The organization's long-term success is directly related to that integration.

The following are familiar examples of this dynamic.

APPLE—Leveraging Innovation Opportunities

Innovation has always been Apple's strength, from its first computer on a board, to the Apple 2, to the Mac and onwards to the iPod, iPhone, iPad, iWatch etc.

However, without their expertise in operations effectiveness they could not have been able to ship millions of quality units, always at a profit.

Product design, ease of use, the concept of apps effectively customizing each device for each customer, has driven an elevated level of customer satisfaction.

The agility in creating the Apple store to meet the service and support requirements of its huge customer base and the company's focus on engaging and educating its staff are exemplary examples of its Organization Agility and Learning Culture.

WAL-MART—Leveraging Operational Effectiveness

WAL-MART leveraged the use of technology in distribution and operations to spur their success.

They turned their volume buying power in negotiating lowest prices from suppliers into savings for their customers. That and the availability of goods on their shelves has gained them an elevated level of customer satisfaction.

All their people are called Associates, emphasizing their involvement and they encourage a team environment in each location.

Challenged by the success of Internet based suppliers in virtually all their product categories, they have continued to embrace their business model and are making acquisitions to be able to succeed in a very competitive retail environment.

IBM—Leveraging Organization Agility

IBM's long-term success was often driven by watching others in their areas of expertise and once they saw their success, they not only entered those markets, but in many cases, dominated them. Mini computers, home computers, application software, technology management services being an example of their business agility.

Their historic investment in management training has spurred a very high level of retained loyalty, even from ex-employees, which has contributed to their growth as these executives played significant roles in the other organizations that they joined or created; and of course, provided IBM itself with top level leadership.

In the arena of large scale computers, IBM is the leader in developing advanced technologies for dealing with very complex issues. Their recent full commitment to Artificial Intelligence is stimulating a whole new world of Innovation.

Their practice of quarterly face-to-face meetings with all their major customers has been a key factor in maintaining customer loyalty and understanding their needs.

AMAZON—Leveraging Customer Satisfaction (reference Appendix 1)

Jeff Bezos has driven the art of Customer Satisfaction to such a level that Amazon is rated at the top of the ladder in that category.

To achieve that status, they are continually running multiple research initiatives to find innovative and better ways to service customers and satisfy their needs.

Bezos has created an environment of continuous operational improvement in everything they do to deliver best value and service for their customers.

The continuous improvement culture at Amazon is based on the Four Pillars of: customer centricity, continuous optimization, a culture of innovation and corporate agility. He has leveraged these to expand his business not only in selling more product categories but into new business opportunities as well, including their successful cloud based business.

MARRIOTT—Leveraging its Learning Culture

"Take care of your people and they will take care of your customers." This is the #1 rule that John Willard Marriott lived by in building one of the most successful hotel chains in the world.

Marriott got to where he did in the business world by relying on a formidable team of colleagues and employees around him. By caring about their people's needs to grow and learn, and giving them direct training or opportunities to learn new skills and competencies, they have created an environment that has nourished continuous development.

In a service oriented business such as theirs, staff contact with their guests is very high. An engaged staff cares about all aspects of their company including the satisfaction of their guests, the quality and efficiency of their services, being innovative in the services that they offer to maintain their leadership and the ability to assure that the company adapts to change.

CHAPTER 6

DELIVERING ACTIONABLE RESULTS

John Smith an engineer at ABC Corporation received an invitation to participate in a customer improvement survey from his supplier BESTCO. Being familiar with such requests, as ABC also runs annual customer satisfaction surveys, he accepted the invitation and was transferred onto the survey site.

He knew it was coming, having received a request a day earlier from BESTCO's CEO about it, and encouraging his participation.

The instructions were very simple and following a quick review he continued to do the survey.

It took him under 5 minutes to answer the questions that he was requested to score from 0 – 10, from poor to excellent.

That section followed with a few open-ended questions mainly related to things that BESTCO could do to improve their relationship with his company.

Having had to complete many other surveys which always asked many more questions and often took over 30 minutes to do, he was impressed by how easy it was to complete and he was finished in just over 7 minutes.

John's company was among 30 other companies in the International division that responded to the survey. At the same time 50 customers from the North American division responded to the survey.

In all the cases, each respondent not only rated BESTCO, but how BESTCO compared to all the other suppliers that they dealt with.

What did BESTCO learn? How did they benefit.

- Because John rated all its Essential Capabilities, he communicated which ones he thought BESTCO was good at—rating them 7 or higher, which ones that he thought were OK but average (5–7), and which he thought could do with a lot of improvement (>5).

- In analyzing his results BESTCO could immediately identify, the specific Essential Capabilities that ABC rated them highly on, and those that they thought could be better.

- By looking at the questions that John rated the lowest, BESTCO had an indication of what would help increase ABC's loyalty to them as related to that element.

John was impressed to get a call from his BESTCO sales representative several weeks later, appreciating his participation and exploring with him why John had rated some of the elements as he had. It was a frank conversation and John felt good about how serious BESTCO was in learning more about his point of view. Although they also did annual surveys, John knew that his company did little if any, follow-ups with their customers.

- By looking at the average of all the Essential Capabilities, they understood the loyalty rating of John's company. As a business BESTCO was aiming to have all their customers loyalty rating exceed 7 out of 10.

- BESTCO analyzed all the results from the combined averages of the 30 International customers and all 50 North American ones (defined as the wisdom of the crowd). It immediately told them which of all their Essential Capabilities each division's customers considered them good at and which could benefit from improvement. It quantified the goodwill of the customers as well as how they rated BESTCO as a brand.

- It allowed BESTCO to understand how their staff was perceived by their customers—effectively evaluating their perspective on BESTCO's culture, the company's innovation orientation and ability to adapt to change.

- Comparing the divisions, allowed BESTCO to identify which positive business practices each had and see if there were approaches that were transferable. In addition, it allowed the company to undertake specific initiatives suited for each division.

....

Bob Harris, BESTCO's International Divisions Marketing manager, along with all the other International Divisions managers were also invited to participate. In addition to the Managers at the North American Division, the top executives of the company, participated as a group.

Bob was concerned about expressing his opinions in case it could impact his position and future with the company. When he understood that his results were being handled anonymously, and that his rating would only be part of all the ratings in his division, it made it more comfortable for him to participate.

At the same time, a sampling of employees in each division and at head office, were invited to participate as well. The employees were grouped by their department such as marketing, customer service, operations, and administration. As with the managers, they were comforted by their anonymity and having their ratings combined with others in their department.

What did BESTCO learn? How did they benefit.

- BESTCO could compare how the two sets of Division managers and the Executive group rated their company on its Essential Capabilities. They could identify how each saw those elements that rated highest and those that could use improvement.

- By relating the questions to the scores, it identified possible action initiatives that could be considered for all the managers in both divisions and any specific ones for each division.

- In addition to understand any differences between them, it allowed them to see how the management ratings within each division compared to the employee ratings within that division. Did they see things in the same way and if not, try to understand why? Department ratings may identify which ones functioned better than others and by relating the questions to the scores, what actions could be considered for improvement.

- BESTCO knew that the closer that the ratings were between management and staff, the better it reflected how closely they worked together. Also important was how management and staff related to the customers perspective of the company.

- Being customer focused as a primary business objective was most important to the company, but satisfying customer needs and requirements was the task of the management and their teams. The Essential Capabilities ratings allowed the executive and management to make changes that would improve the customer ratings and directly influence growth and profitability.

Relating The HALO Effect quantification of Essential Capabilities to various business issues.

Which of these factors relates to your business today?

Issue based factors

Most businesses tackle any issues that arise on a one by one basis. Energy and resources are allocated to "fix" each one as they occur. It sounds logical, and often works in resolving that issue. However, the source cause of the issue may not have been isolated and re-occurrence can happen. Also, the implications on other aspects of the business through that initiative may not be realized, resulting in other issue based challenges to arise.

Quantifying the specific Essential Capability related to the issue involved at the time and relating it to all the company's other Essential Capabilities provides a baseline related to that issue, and often may identify potential causes. Once the corrective actions are taken, the change in the value of the related Essential Capabilities and the impact on all the others can be assessed and actions identified to assure that they are adjusted accordingly.

As an example: let's say that the company has seen its gross margins eroding somewhat over the last few years. Measuring the company's Essential Capabilities, may identify issues related to operating costs, and/or competitive factors, and/ or marketing issues. Applying a "fix" to the issue that was identified as the primary one is logical. By evaluating the post results to see if that was the right decision is valuable, and if it had any implications on all the other Essential Capabilities would certainly be prudent.

A classic story is what happened to the Cadillac Division of General Motors many years ago. Cadillac had such an incredible reputation at one time that its name was synonymous in branding any product or service as "the best, the top standard"–"to be like Cadillac" was a desired statement. To increase profitability, the new head of the company at that time decided on implementing significant cost reduction measures including in the vehicle itself. For the first year it worked and profits rose. However, the changes caused quality issues that it had never had before. Within a few years it resulted in destroying their brand reputation, greatly impacted their sales, and damaged their long–term profitability. They lost sight of their brand identity and values, from which they never recovered.

The **loyalty of your customers** is another **basic issue and survival need** for every company. Many companies do customer surveys. If you add understanding the customer perspective of your company's Essential Capabilities, you gain the additional insight on what your customers desire to maintain and increase their loyalty.

Growth based factors

Successful long-term businesses strive to have a culture of innovation. A culture that drives thinking of new and better ways to service its customers and develop products and services to expand its markets. The quantification of the Essential Capabilities of the company will identify what barriers the company must overcome to achieve such a position.

It answers questions such as the motivation of its staff to be involved in improving the business; how adaptive the company is to change; how closely it works with its customers in helping with their success. Innovation is driven by every aspect of a business and having insight on where to focus in creating a culture of innovation is essential.

If growth is related to the acquisition of a firm, or to a merger, knowing the quantification of the Essential Capabilities of that firm in advance, and how it will fit with yours are important criteria to improve the success of the acquisition, and minimize any integration issues in the case of a merger.

Exit based factors

The primary interest in your company, should you want to exit the business, is its value to the buyer or stock market if that is a desired direction. That value has multiple components that are beyond your financial data of sales and profitability. They include succession planning, the brand value that your business has; the goodwill of your customers; the loyalty of your key staff; the effectiveness of your management; the efficiency of your operations; your businesses innovation orientation, amongst others. None of the above being quantifiably visible in your balance sheet, yet crucial for the buyer or investor.

Knowing the quantification of the Essential Capabilities of your company in advance of any planned exit undertaking and knowing what to do with strengthening the above factors will greatly impact your companies value to any buyer or successor. It may also have a side effect in that by making the multiple positive changes, the fortunes of the business may possibly make you to reconsider the exit strategy being considered.

The Balanced Scorecard by Kaplan and Norton outlined a methodology for managing change in organizations and became a favorite for many enterprises. As it required an understanding of the strategic objectives of each business, customization for each one was necessary. It was a significant undertaking, often involving outside consulting services along with the involvement of management and staff to both implement and monitor.

The HALO Effect methodology, being a technology driven universal diagnostic is an ideal front end for The Balanced Scorecard, and any business management methodologies that are similar. It provides a quick non-intrusive means to establish a high-level baseline for the non-financial operational performance of the enterprise, identifying where changes can be taken through applications such as that of The Balanced Scorecard, and establishes a means to measure and monitor the success of such actions. It also provides a means to benchmark each organization to others in its sector and industry.

CHAPTER 7

ADDITIONAL VALIDATION AND EXAMPLES OF HOW THE HALO EFFECT CAN BE APPLIED

As outlined in Chapter 3, it was the substantial number of diverse ways that the methodology was being applied by businesses of diverse types and sizes that prompted my analogy of it to the Essential Capabilities as related to the effect of knowing and mapping a person's DNA.

The following are actual business case applications of the adaptability of the methodology to various situations.

CASE STUDY–OF ITS VALUE FOR CONTINUOUS IMPROVEMENT:

BACKGROUND

One of the independent operating subsidiaries of a major Global conglomerate in the construction and related services field has been utilizing the Essential Capabilities methodology annually for the last five years.

The newly appointed CEO at the time of first use was challenged by a company that was losing money and struggling.

Based on the metrics that the conglomerate used to gauge each of its 16 divisions and direct subsidiaries, his company ranked amongst the poorer ones.

A business friend recommended him using the methodology that the friend was familiar with. He advised the CEO that he thought it would be a good start as a basis for him to capture an overview of the strengths and weaknesses of the company that he was now responsible for.

PROCESS & ACTIONS

Within four weeks of contacting our company and contracting for the process, the CEO received the report. He later said he was amazed on how easy it was to get the process underway, the fast response that came from it, and most importantly the resulting information.

The CEO brought his top management team together and shared the report with them.

In addition to understanding the differences on how his customers and suppliers rated them as compared to the management and employees–an enlightening experience for the management team, the report identified the company's overall weaknesses along several important capabilities. It also identified some strengths to build on. The weaknesses included issues with communications with customers and suppliers, and with the effectiveness of the management team.

Based on specific areas that the report identified, the management team brainstormed various solutions and selected a series of initiatives to correct them.

The process was repeated the following four years, each time evaluating the impact of the initiatives that they had undertaken, and identifying new capabilities that required improvement.

OUTCOME

Over a 5-year period, the overall Essential Capabilities scores went from 6.7 up to 8, with sales increasing from **US$24M to $60M annually**, and EBT from **-1% to 6.7%**. The CEO attributed his subsidiary's improved sales, customer and supplier satisfaction and resulting bottom-line success, in no small way, to The HALO Effect quantification methodology.

Since 2016 his subsidiary has been ranked by corporate as the highest in performance amongst all 16 in the company.

CASE STUDY–OF ITS APPLICATION IN DUE DILIGENCE:

BACKGROUND

A Private Equity (PE) firm was in the final stages of closing an acquisition of a manufacturing company. All the financial and marketing due-diligence was complete, and although they had contacted a few of the company's customers and received positive feedback from them, they decided to utilize The HALO Effect methodology to get feedback from a much larger number of that company's customers.

Timing was important as both parties were anxious to close the deal.

PROCESS & ACTIONS

A joinder non-disclosure agreement was signed with the acquiring firm to assure the full confidentiality of the process, and as comfort to the targeted company. The target company, agreed to providing the contact information of 50 of their most active customers under the condition that the company names would not be revealed to the acquiring firm.

The company issued an e-mail to all the potential contacts advising them that they were being surveyed as part of a business improvement initiative by an independent company, and requesting their co-operation, when receiving the invitation from that firm.

OUTCOME

More than half of the customers responded to the invitations sent within the following 5 working days, an extremely valid statistical sample size.

The results that were delivered a few days later showed that 52% rated their loyalty to the company as being below average. They rated the company weak in innovation, and the involvement of their people. Although they rated well in Operations Effectiveness, Customer satisfaction and Agility were just average.

Based on the results, the PE firm substantially changed the terms of the deal, which resulted in it being terminated.

CASE STUDY–OF ITS VALUE IN A MERGER OR ACQUISITION

BACKGROUND

Coming up after 11 months following the merger of two companies in the same industry, things were not going well, and the wisdom of the merger was in question. The pre-merger objective of leveraging the combined scale and reducing the duplication of overheads to greatly increase profitability was having the opposite effect. Margins had dropped and internal staff issues resulted in key personnel leaving. In addition, multiple technology integration issues had arisen and were impacting customer both operations and deliveries.

PROCESS & ACTIONS

The consultant brought in to determine what had to be done. He immediately implemented The HALO Effect methodology. In its design, he split the customers into two groups, based on their original company affiliations, he did likewise with several of the key departments, separating the staff within them by their original company affiliation. Open-ended questions added, requested input on how each grouping felt about certain functions before and after the merger.

OUTCOME

In general, the report results outlined very different ratings on most of the 15 Essential Capabilities from each of the original groupings from both organizations. The orientation of one of them highlighted a strong internally focused attitude re: Operations and Agility, along with high ratings for employee involvement and teamwork. Whereas the other highlighted an externally focused orientation re: Customer Satisfaction and Innovation, and a weak culture.

The consultant noted that the new leadership did not recognize these issues and that most came from the company that were stronger on their external orientation. A major senior management restructuring was implemented as a result.

The first of two-consecutive annual undertakings on the re-organized entity demonstrated that improvements were taking hold; an improvement in the engagement of their staff, along with sales and margin growth.

CASE STUDY–OF ITS VALUE IN A RESTRUCTURING/ TURNAROUND

BACKGROUND

Two brothers who loved making things, started a custom design plastics company in their garage. As they got to be known, they expanded into their own plant. They were profitable and grew the business by employing friends and relatives. After the city newspaper interviewed them and wrote up a very complimentary article, business picked up considerably, and things started going downhill. Customer orders were falling behind, many quality issues appeared creating unexpected rework. Costs increased dramatically and they started losing money.

PROCESS & ACTIONS

They retained a consultant recommended by a friend. He immediately instituted The HALO Effect methodology, while simultaneously meeting the key staff and evaluating their operating systems. The report feedback clearly identified serious leadership and management issues, amongst many others. This confirmed his finding that both the brothers and the people that they had set-up as managers and supervisors, had no previous background in those capacities. Customer feedback indicated a very low level of loyalty, with many of them clearly stating that they would not be using the company again due to the quality and delivery problems. The employees as well, were discouraged and they were concerned about the company survival.

With their permission, he took over the company leadership with a one-year contract. He had one of the brothers, the one that he felt could be a leader become his assistant, while the other, a technically competent person, registered for a series of manufacturing related courses at the local university. Within two months from taking over, and having replaced most of the managers with a new team of managers, he organized a two-day off-site weekend.

Using the report, as the guide, they brainstormed and determined a series of changes that needed to be done over the following six months. They also set a target for customer satisfaction that they all felt was important to achieve.

OUTCOME
They repeated the methodology six months and 12 months later. The first showed a modest improvement, during which time the quality and delivery issues were greatly improved. By the time of the termination of his contract, sales were growing, the company became profitable, the brother that was his assistant, became President, while the other brother became

the VP of Manufacturing. The consultant, joined the Advisory Board of the company, along with their Accountant.

CHAPTER 8

IN CLOSING

If you can't measure it, you can't improve it." **Peter Drucker**

All companies utilize financial data in such exercises—sales, margins, profits, etc. These change indicators are historic in nature, whether by last month, quarter or year. To monitor ongoing operational changes, most companies rely on Key Performance Indicators (KPIs). These may include units produced, shipped, returns, line stoppages, virtually hundreds that can be employed in a practical way within any company. These are very valuable for day to day monitoring of specific and critical business functions.

Leveraging the quantification of the Essential Capabilities of any business, The HALO Effect is the first methodology that allows companies to monitor their overall operational performance quickly, objectively and economically. It not only reflects the business performance status at the time it is executed, but it also identifies opportunities that can impact the company's future through its insights into the company's brand, the goodwill of its customers, the organization's culture, the effectiveness of its management, the alignment of all its stakeholders, and critically, what its customers require for retaining and increasing their loyalty.

Just like as a person who weighs himself or herself every day to maintain and at times act on changing weight, the quantification of its Essential Capabilities plays the same role in a business.

The discipline required, however, is essential for any long-term sustainable success. Jeff Bezos, Sam Walton and those others who have built strong, well-established and growing organizations are a testament to the discipline that leadership must bring to organizations that want to do the same.

THE POWER OF THE HALO EFFECT METHODOLOGY

The HALO Effect methodology is a next-generation resource for organizations seeking an instrument that meets the twin objectives of providing an assessment of what is and providing feedback that can mobilize toward what ought to be.

The methodology presents a comprehensive and integrated picture of the organization. It provides numerous direct, indirect and comparison measures of organization strengths, weaknesses, opportunities and threats. In addition, it facilitates the management of desired change throughout the organization.

The HALO Effect methodology is a new paradigm for implementing a program of continuous organization improvement and growth, organization adaptation to change, creating a culture of innovation, delighting customers and organization learning. It delivers objective, measurable benchmarks efficiently and economically, making this resource accessible to any size and type of organization. The methodology serves as a galvanizing event stimulating the entire organization to pay attention to stakeholder feedback. It goes beyond any typical survey, or other data gathering means to offer the organization a learning experience in organizational self-transformation.

As a definitive measure of all the non-financial operational performance of any organization, the quantification of its Essential Capabilities can take on many roles.

- Effectively listening to customers and identifying what needs to be done to delight them and monitoring how they react to the changes made;

- Identifying the barriers to growing the company;
- Providing quantifiable data that is not available on any balance sheet
- Understanding the strengths and weaknesses on a target company, and reducing risk of an investment in the due diligence process in a pending investment or acquisition;
- Dealing with the unfortunately frequent post merger surprises by understanding the strengths and weaknesses of each company;
- Identifying the barriers for creating a culture of innovation in businesses;
- Providing an assessment of the organization oriented training requirements;
- Providing independent feedback for directors and investors on the progress on their companies.

APPENDICIES

APPENDIX I

UNDERSTANDING AMAZON'S SUCCESS

Jeff Bezos did not know about The HALO Effect methodology when he started his company. He may still not know about it over 20 years later. Yet intuitively he has become one of the leading examples of the implementation of all the principles and designs of the methodology.

Jeff is not the only one who has traveled the same path without any knowledge of our methodology. There are many more success stories of companies who have done likewise. Unfortunately, in the context of millions of businesses, his and the other truly equivalent success stories are extremely few.

Jeff believed that by creating a business whose mission was 100% focused on customer delight, would lead him to be successful. He could not walk the talk however, without the full engagement of every aspect of his company.

The HALO Effect methodology is the theoretical embodiment of the 4 Pillars that Jeff Bezos has intuitively institutionalized in making his company so successful.

The process-ideal of continuous improvement serves as a direction for organization action, not as an endpoint. Amazon under Jeff Bezos leadership embodies those characteristics. Ideals are ultimate standards, never 100% attainable. Amazon's continued success will be dictated by how well they continue that pursuit.

The HALO Effect methodology, allows any company of any type and size, to measure and evaluate its business on the same Pillars as Amazon, but with a level of detail within each Pillar that can be converted into action initiatives for improvement. Leveraging technology and the Internet, it presents objective and easy to interpret feedback in the form of analytics economically, quickly—within days and is non-invasive.

The arrival of one of the best business books written in the longest long time: *Be Like Amazon—Even a Lemonade Stand can do It,* by Bryan and Jeffery Eisenberg and Roy Williams, demonstrates how understanding the four Pillars can be applied to any company. Allowing companies to rate themselves on the four Pillars of Amazon's success, a free evaluation utilizing The

HALO Effect methodology has been employed by them to stimulate any business of any type and size to try and emulate what Jeff Bezos has done.

APPENDIX 2

THE GENESIS OF THE METHODOLOGY

The major global recession in 1991 greatly impacted the successful management development company that my late business partner Max Garfinkle (1928–1999) and I had created in 1984. The experience however, stimulated us to understand why we failed, given our services were highly rated by major corporations. The consensus in talking to our clients was that although we were helping individual managers, we needed to contribute to the overall success of the businesses.

So how would we do that? We decided to initiate some research on organizations. Led by Max, this initiative ended being a major multi-year undertaking.

The base assumption was that although businesses are all different, there must be common characteristics that apply to all of them. With the collaboration of several of our major clients, our research identified five unique organization-oriented strategic challenges1 that were common to all of them, and by inference, to all enterprises. As we uncovered these, we identified multiple organization capabilities that supported each one of them. Through a process of distillation of the research and feedback from our clients, we isolated the most significant capabilities for each one, which led us to creating a universal methodology to quantify them.

We were then faced with the challenge of how to prove its value to businesses as an ongoing resource.

The task seemed straight forward—find a few customers that would value the initial feedback that it delivered, undertake changes in the organization that were identified and then run it again and evaluate the impact of these actions on the company's success, especially on its improvement to the bottom line. Along with the challenge of finding willing customers to try it out, the management of those customers had to want to use the feedback to act. That, and a reluctance on their part to provide financial feedback, turned out to be challenges that took a long time to overcome.

During one of our morning walk and talk sessions, several years after launching our business and having seen the effect that our methodology had on multiple businesses, I said **"Max, we may have uncovered the universal DNA of business!"**

What an audacious statement to make. How can one compare the "hidden language of cells"—the three-billion-unit code that identifies our human DNA to quantifying the Essential Capabilities that form the elements of the map of organizations that Max and I developed?

Relating the Human Genome Project, a huge international effort involving thousands of scientists, spearheaded by the US government and working at decoding human life, to the research we did on organizations, may seem ridiculous. Even if one understands that we tackled a meta-analysis of the literature, which considered the knowledge, wisdom and insights developed by many others, it still seems illogical to compare our efforts to the Human Genome Project.

Max dismissed my statement immediately. I agreed, but recognized the unique capabilities of our methodology as a universal resource that can help businesses in so many ways.

APPENDIX 3

ABOUT MAX GARFINKLE

In 1993, Max Garfinkle and I co-founded Capability Snapshot Inc., the original name of CSI Diagnostics Inc.

Our business relationship began in 1984 when the two of us founded a management-consulting firm with offices in Montreal, Toronto, and Boston that specialized in one-to-one coaching of senior managers. The practice focused on strategic thinking, team leadership and self-awareness. Managers were accompanied by consulting "coaches" as they implemented programs of continuous improvement and organization transformation.

We had known each other for over thirty-four years. Besides our business relationship, he was my mentor and coach. He was a visionary who never accepted the status quo. He always strove for the ideal, and encouraged others to do the same. Even in the darkest days of our voyage, and there were quite a few, he maintained that perspective and would try for solutions that challenged normal conventions.

Max was born and educated in Montreal. He received his B. Sc. degree from Sir George Williams (Concordia) University. He acquired his Ph. D. degree from Columbia University, with a specialization in Counseling Psychology, and completed his internship year at the Counseling Center of the University of California at Berkeley, California.

Max had worked as an Industrial/Organizational psychologist with a large supermarket chain in Montreal. He pioneered the creation of a "training store", where an actual store was used as a learning laboratory for training store managers. His memos on strategy to the president contributed to the company's rapid and successful expansion.

Max had been an Associate Professor in the Department of Psychology at the "University of Montréal". He directed the research projects of numerous master's and doctoral students, focusing on qualitative research that emphasized relevance to practical applications. During that time, he served as the Coordinator of Graduate Studies in Applied Psychology. He also organized and chaired the first Canadian conference on Community Psychology on behalf of the Canadian Psychological Association.

Max loved research. He had the ability to rapidly scan books and articles, and quickly grasp their essence. He could quote verbatim, material from those books and articles that he valued. Max loved bookstores and libraries. He made several trips each year to New York where he would spend several full days on each trip at one of his favourite bookstores, the Strand. He would return with dozens of books and pages of notes on each trip. Max drew his research from many disciplines, as is attested in the material presented and in the attached section on Research.

He often quoted Sir Isaac Newton in saying that "he stood on the shoulders of giants".

In addition to my role in challenging his ideas, and adding my business and technology expertise, Max collaborated with many of his academic and industry colleagues, all of which aided in turning theory into a practical resource.

When Max and I started on the road of the Essential Capabilities for businesses methodology in the early1990's, we never anticipated it taking so long, or being so difficult a path. As natural optimists, we both had expectations of achieving market acceptance within a few, meaning 2 to 5 years. We have walked and lived a true entrepreneurial journey, with the ups and downs, the near collapses, and the euphoric highs that come, at times, from the smallest successes.

APPENDIX 4:

THE RESEARCH

The following quotation from Arthur Koestler is very appropriate in relation to the development of The HALO Effect and explains what was done to develop something that never existed before, and for that matter, since.

"The more original the discovery the more obvious it seems afterwards"

The research bibliography below is organized around key topic areas:

- ON HIGHER-PERFORMING, AGILE, LEARNING ORGANIZATIONS
- ON THE FIVE GENERIC "STRATEGIC CHALLENGES"

- ON THE THREE "ESSENTIAL CAPABILITIES" FOR EACH CHALLENGE
- ON THE POWER OF THE FRAMEWORK
- ON FEEDBACK, COLLECTING, PROCESSING, SELECTING GROUPS and SAMPLE SIZES
- ON UNDERSTANDING THE STRATEGY OF THE ORGANIZER INQUIRY
- ON COMPARISON OF PERSPECTIVES
- ON ORGANIZATION SENSEMAKING
- ON ORGANIZATION LEARNING
- ON ORGANIZATION STRIVING and ENERGISING

The following represent a sampling of the literature that was reviewed for each of the applicable topic areas. In addition, numerous academic papers and articles from leading journals were also referenced.

ON HIGHER-PERFORMING, AGILE, LEARNING ORGANIZATIONS

Ackoff, Russell L., Creating the Corporate Future, Wiley, 1981

Collins, Porras, Built to Last, Harper Business, 1991

Gibson, Rethinking the Future, Bealey Publishing, 1997

Goldman, Nagel, Preiss, Agile Competitors and Virtual Organizations, Van Nostrand Reinhold, 1995

Hackman, Oldham, Work Redesign, Addison-Wesley, 1980

Handy, Charles, The Age of Unreason Harvard Business School Press, 1989

Hendry, Johnson, Newton, Strategic Thinking, Wiley, 1993

McGill, Slocum, The Smarter Organization, Wiley, 1994

Peters, Tom, Thriving on Chaos, Knopf, 1987

Quinn, James Brian, Intelligent Enterprise, Free Press, 1992

Senge, Peter, The Fifth Discipline: The Art and Practice of the Learning Organization, Doubleday, 1996

Slaughter, Richard A, The Foresight Principle, Praeger, 1995

ON THE FIVE GENERIC "STRATEGIC CHALLENGES"

Abell, Derek F., Managing with Dual Strategies, The Free press, 1993

Hamel Prahald, Competing for the Future, Harvard Business School Press, 1994

Heene, Competence-Based Competition, John Wiley & Sons, 1994

Mintzberg, Henry The Rise and Fall of Strategic Planning, Free Press, 1994

Porter, Michael E., Competitive Advantage, Free Press, 1985

Treacy, Wiersema, Discipline of Market Leaders, Addison-Wesley, 1995

ON THE THREE *ESSENTIAL CAPABILITIES* FOR EACH CHALLENGE

Cushman, King, Communication and High-speed Management, State University of New York Press, 1995

Hamel, Heene, Competence-Based Competition, John Wiley & Sons, 1994

Stalk, Evans, Shulman, Competing on Capabilities, Harvard Business Review, 1992

Walton, Sam Made In America, Doubleday, 1992

ON THE POWER OF THE FRAMEWORK

Davis, Stanley M., Future Perfect, Addison-Wesley, 1987

Ghoshal, Bartlett, The Individual Organization, Harper business, 1997

Jaques, Clement, Executive Leadership, Cason Hall, 1991

Kouzes, Posner, The Leadership Challenge, Jossey-Bass, 1987

Kotter, John P., A Force for Change, Free Press, 1990

ON FEEDBACK, COLLECTING, PROCESSING, SELECTING GROUPS and SAMPLE SIZES

Bryman A, Research Methods and Organization Studies, Routledge, 1989

Gergen, Kenneth J., Toward transformation in Social Knowledge, Sage, 1994

Guba, Egon G., The Paradigm Dialog, Sage, 1990

Krueger, Richard A., Focus Groups, Sage, 1988

Miles, Huberman, Qualitative Data Analysis, Sage, 1994

Nadler, David A, Feedback and Organizational Development, Addison-Wesley, 1977

Naumann, Giel, Customer Satisfaction Measurement and Management, Thomson Executive Press, 1995

ON UNDERSTANDING THE STRATEGY OF THE ORGANIZER INQUIRY

Howard, Ann, Diagnosis for Organizational Change, Guilford, 1994

Ghoshal, Bartlett, The Individual Organization, Harper business, 1997

Guba, Egon G., The Paradigm Dialog, Sage, 1990

Kaplan, Norton, The Balanced Scorecard, Harvard Business School Press, 1996

Morgan, Garath, Images of Organization, Sage, 1986

Nadler, David A, Feedback and Organizational Development, Addison-Wesley, 1977

Poirier, Houser, Business Partnering for Continuous Improvement, Berrett-Koehler, 1993

Torbert, William R., Managing the Corporate Dream, Dow Jones-Irwin, 1987

Torbert, William R., The Balance of Power, Sage, 1991

Torres, Preskill, Piontek Evaluation Strategies for Communicating and Reporting, Sage, 1966

ON COMPARISON OF PERSPECTIVES

Adler, Nancy J., Organization Behavior, Wadsworth, 1991

Ghoshal, Bartlett, The Individual Organization, Harper business, 1997

Hall, Johnson, Turney, Measuring Up, Business One Irwin, 1996

Nahser, Byron F., Learning to Read the Signs, Butterworth-Heinemann, 1997

Reichheld, Frederick, F The Loyalty Effect, Harvard Business School Press, 1996

ON ORGANIZATION SENSEMAKING

Berger, Luckmann, The Social Construction of Reality, Anchor,

Bradley, Nolan, Sense and Respond, Harvard Business School Press,

Gergen, Kenneth J., Toward transformation in Social Knowledge, Sage,

Morgan, Garath, Images of Organization, Sage,

Weick, Karl E., Sense-making in Organizations, Sage,

ON ORGANIZATION LEARNING

Argyris, Schon, Organization Learning, Addison-Wesley, 1978

Savage, Charles M, 5th Generation Management Butter-worth-Heinemann, 1996,

Heckscher, Donnellson, Post-Bureaucratic Organization, Sage, 1994

Kegan, Robert, In Over Our Heads, Harvard University Press, 1994

McCall, Lombardo, Morrison, The Lessons of Experience, 1988

Mintzberg, Henry, Structure in Fives – Designing Effective Organizations, Prentice-Hall, 1983

Preiss, Goldman, Nagel, Cooperate to Compete, Van Nostrand Reinhold, 1996

Slywotzky, Adrian J., Value Migration, Harvard Business Press, 1996

Slywotzky, Morrison, How Strategic Business Design will Lead You to Tomorrow's Profits, Time Business, 1997

ON ORGANIZATION STRIVING and ENERGISING

Hamel, Heene, Competence-Based Competition, John Wiley & Sons, 1994

Heskett, Sasser, Schlesinger, The Service Profit Chain, Free Press, 1997

Itami, Roehl, Mobilizing Invisible Assets, Harvard University Press, 1983

Kanter, Rosabeth Moss, The Change Masters, Simon and Shuster, 1983

Kanter, Rosabeth Moss, When Giants Learn to Dance, Simon and Shuster, 1989

Wiersema, Fred, Customer Intimacy, Knowledge Exchange, 1996

ABOUT THE AUTHOR

This is the first book from Jerry Tarasofsky.

Jerry Tarasofsky is a serial entrepreneur; an organization and management development consultant; a creative thinker; a challenger of the status-quo and for over 55 years a technology aficionado.

Upon graduating with both a Science and Arts degree from Concordia University in Montreal in 1962/63, Jerry worked in several large companies — Alcan, ITT, Kruger and Air Liquid, starting as a system's analyst and becoming head of IT at Air Liquid.

Following those jobs, he founded or co-founded multiple businesses:

- Rapatax, one of the world's first attempt at a commercial business utilizing time-sharing technology;

- Compucentre, the world's first chain of computer and advanced electronic stores
- JT&A Consulting, introducing early-stage on-line applications, creating multiple business applications for the mini-computer industry;
- Mage Centers for Management Development, one of the first individual management coaching businesses with offices in Boston, Toronto and Montreal;
- iPerceptions, the world's first voice-of-customer analytics platform, and
- CSI Diagnostics, his current business.

He serves on the Board of Directors for public, private and non-profit organizations.

Jerry is married to Elaine; father of Robert, Daniel and Janet; and grandfather to Joshua, Rachel and Ayla.

www.ingramcontent.com/pod-product-compliance
Lightning Source LLC
Chambersburg PA
CBHW071521200326
41519CB00019B/6023

* 9 7 8 1 9 8 8 9 9 4 0 4 8 *